desecrated poppies

Yaffa

Copyright © 2024

All rights reserved

Published in 2024 by Meraj Publishing

1st Paperback Edition

This is a work of creative nonfiction. Some parts have been fictionalized in varying degrees, for various purposes.

No part of this book may be reproduced or used in any manner without written permission of the copyright owner except for the use of quotations in a book review. For more information, address: info@merajpublishing.com

ISBN: 979-8-9894734-3-4 (Paperback)

ISBN: 979-8-9894734-4-1 (Ebook)

Cover art by Yaffa AS

Exterior and Interior layout by Andrea Ramos Campos

merajpublishing.com

To the forgotten trans people killed in genocides – whose names, stories, and even numbers will never be known.

To the trans people who survive fascist genocide every day. We are divine.

We will never know how many trans Palestinians have been killed in Gaza since October 7th, let alone their names and stories. We say "never again" and "we will not forget," but that does not include trans people when we never remembered them to begin with. This applies to every genocide, every war, every trans person killed by settler colonialism. Remembering trans people is different; it is a state of being, with no names or stories, but an understanding that transness has always existed. Our bodily autonomy is interlinked with Indigenous sovereignty and the end of settler colonialism.

This mural is a way of remembering the thirteen trans Palestinians who were killed in Gaza that Mx. Yaffa knew, symbolized by thirteen poppies flying in the wind beyond the rubble left behind. The poppies are transparent, moving beyond what we perceive as life. Amidst the rubble, fully colored poppies represent the trans Palestinians still claiming life. The names surrounding the mural are those of Yaffa's family members who have been killed since October 7, 2023.

The mural was displayed at the National Queer Arts Fest in June 2024. For a color photograph of the mural & the digital prints, visit the QR code or link below.

https://www.merajpublishing.com/desecrated-poppies

transness, like
indigeneity, like
Blackness, like
Palestine
is the weapon
that will usher in
the new age of
Fascism

it's harder to
write about Falasteen
these days

after knowing names
of family, friends

after death shrouded
all we are
injustice claiming
what is not theirs

easier when the pain
was fresh, still hadn't
stained

easier when it
was the only
purpose
every word
a final hope

harder on an
endless road
50+ tour dates
two books
thousands
of people

harder as the eclipse
retreats
aries calling us to
war

We need a Trans and Black Led Palestinian movement if we are going to counter fascism

As of June 6th, 2024, there are currently 557 anti-trans bills across 42 states, 45 national bills to block trans people from any and all human rights. There are currently 293 anti-Palestinian bills. The bills have many things in common. They impact far more people than just the hated identities listed on them. They are crafted by the exact same people. They move us towards fascism. The same can be said about cop cities, anti-abortion bills, and so many others that white christian nationalists are moving forward.

In a political system where both major parties are pro-genocide and pro-fascism which do you choose?

Many compare the 2024 elections with the 2016 elections. Although many of us knew the pro-genocide nature of democrats in 2016, the current genocide in Palestine has ensured that this pillar of the democrats' foundation is undeniable.

Over the last 8 years, as trans global majority folks we have seen the conservative and liberal democrats both moving towards the right out of sheer hatred for transness. The conservative Muslim community said so in a statement released by Al-Yaqeen Institute in June 2023, saying:

"Consistent with our claim of non-partisanship, we are committed to working with individuals of all religious and political affiliations to protect the constitutional right of faith communities to live according to their religious convictions and to uphold justice for all." [1]

This statement, is perhaps one of the most visual representations of the behind the scenes allyship between the far-right and different conservative marginalized identities. This did not happen overnight, this has been in the works for years, and the question of "who do you hate more?" has been a consideration for several decades. The mainstream far right has always been willing to sacrifice their own rights for the sake of preventing the rights of others, restructuring education, healthcare, and so much more in the 70s and 80s to prevent Black people benefitting from the same access afforded to white communities prior to then.

Democrats and Republicans both share this same philosophy, harm the masses for the benefit of a select few, maintaining systems of oppression at all costs. When the rich and powerful tell others that they can be what they are, that they can be moral, that they can have a purpose, the masses listen, 'democracy' under white imperialism is just another tool like the catholic church and now the evangelist church are. Capitalism tells white people that they're closer to God because their faces are on money in God's image.

This is where the parties also share their vision for fascism. Fascism is usually connected with the far-right in what's known as the united states. Yet, at every opportunity, democrats over the last two decades have only supported the fascist foundation that the right-wing operates from. Fascism is not only a right-wing tool, it is also a major neo-liberal tool. Democrats just know how to gaslight better.

Fascism is a tool of both parties. The liberal elite only got richer during trump, not the opposite. Even as the right wing targets rights that liberal cis-straight white women and cis-white lgbpq+ (Lesbian, Gay, Bisexual, Pansexual, and Queer) members are impacted by; the vast majority of these groups prefer fascism over the global majority. This is only slightly less true for white trans and gender non-conforming individuals. This has been starkly obvious the last eight months in regards to Palestine, during the most visible genocide to ever exist.

Tools such as pinkwashing and purplewashing the use of queer and trans rights and women's rights to further the imperialist colonial project including zionism, are only effective when they validate beliefs that individuals already have. These tools are easy to discredit, and have been easy to discredit throughout the history of the colonial project. It is easy to hold onto beliefs that allow you to continue extracting to maintain a lifestyle that you view can not be maintained otherwise. Here I am not only referring to folks claiming they are of the zionist state, I am referring to all privileged groups who have chosen to assimilate with their privilege instead of fighting alongside the most marginalized for liberation.

Islamophobia, anti-Blackness, and transphobia did not start on October 7th within the liberal LGBPQ+ organizations. The HRC, Trevor project (Boeing), GLAAD (ADL), PFLAG (ADL) and many others did not become complicit in genocide after October 7th, 2023. These organizations have been complicit in every genocide the united states has been supporting for decades, as well as the genocide against Black and trans people in what's known as the united states. These organizations directly receive funds from arms dealers, branding them as saviors in the process.

These organizations, along with the vast majority of pride councils, partner with the same law enforcement offices that have left a trail of Black bodies filled with hundreds of bullets behind. These same organizations partner with and receive funds from the same organizations that benefit from slavery within the prison industrial complex, the same organizations leading to the genocides in the Congo, West Papua, and various other parts of the world, all in the name of capitalism. If you look at the list of companies profiting off of genocide such as the one compiled by the AFSC [2] you will find many orgs are sponsors and partners of pride around what's known as the united states and canada.

Systemic oppression has always known that to maintain power you must establish hierarchies between marginalized groups, elevating one group as you extract more from another. Shifting queer justice to gay marriage is a documented example of this right-wing agenda being adopted by liberals: to elevate some while further marginalizing others. As we move deeper into anti-trans legislation we will be seeing rich and white trans individuals, including celebrity drag artists in the global majority elevated to deflect from the greater consequences that global majority trans people — especially indigenous, Black, and, currently, Palestinian trans people — will be experiencing.

White supremacist tools, whether liberal or right wing, have never changed. Their divide and conquer strategies are still one and the same. In January, when the Queer Palestinian Empowerment Network, under the leadership of Eyad, organized an action during The Taskforces Creating Change conference, the Taskforce leadership weaponized anti-Blackness as a tool to separate the pro-Palestinian organizing group. This tactic failed, due to the solidarity of Black queer and trans people at the conference; it was ultimately indigenous and Black queer and trans femmes who made space for Palestine during the last plenary, allowing me and others to occupy the space.

The fight against fascism is one and the same. However, due to the lack of solidarity from LGBPQ+ orgs and the lack of solidarity from conservative Muslim, Christian, and Jewish Palestinian communities, the movements for trans justice and the movement for Palestinian Indigenous sovereignty have been seen as completely separate despite having shared organizers. Although the pro-Palestine movement is filled with queer and trans individuals, they can rarely name the links between the two forms of justice beyond that none of us are free until we are all free.

Currently, Palestinian and trans identity are the two identities being weaponized to amplify and implement fascist policy. The bills referenced earlier all have consequences to both groups and beyond. Anti-trans policy is anti-Palestine policy and the opposite is true. Both anti-trans and anti-Palestine policy is anti-Black policy. For example, the policies being used to ban queer and trans books are the foundation for the policies that will ban Palestinian history and the mention of Palestine in schools at all. These policies are written in incredibly vague language, allowing them to be weaponized against various groups of people, not only the individuals initially targeted.

We might exist on different wavelengths of marginalization, however, when the source of our oppression is all the same, our survival is tied together. There is no free Falasteen with a fascist state. There are no free trans people within a fascist state. By blocking one road and none of the others, we only detour fascism, we don't prevent it.

On May 10th, 2024 the FBI and DHS issued a public service announcement (PSA) warning that Foreign Terrorist organizations will be targeting Pride this year, citing the Pulse Nightclub Shooting and the arrest of three individuals in Austria in 2023 who 'may' have connections to the Islamic State [3]. Every major news outlet carried the story, this was immediately followed by announcements by various Pride committees announcing increased policing during pride events. These same news outlets have rarely covered the genocide in Palestine, and even fewer have referred to the genocide in Palestine as a genocide.

In my capacity as the Executive Director of the Muslim Alliance for Sexual and Gender Diversity (MASGD), I am conscious of the policies that are targeting us before, during, and after they kill us. As a Palestinian and Black trans-Muslim-led org, we are aware that transness is the identity that is meant to usher in full-on fascism. As Palestinian and Black folks we know that when the police ascend they will kill Black and indigenous folks first. We know that when the government uses the word "terrorist" they mean poor Black Muslims, not people who look like Osama Bin Laden, contrary to what media coverage leads you to believe. Although brownness is surveilled and threatened, we are rarely assassinated. We also know that we operate in a country where our identities are weaponized against other marginalized people, ensuring our separation and continued intra-community harm.

The FBI PSA mentioned earlier about Pride serves as another tool to amplify hierarchies within marginalized communities, further separating us, preventing us from reaching a critical mass that would allow us to prevent and undo the fascist policies being considered. It is imperative, now more than ever to recognize how our survival, more so than just our marginalization, is intrinsically connected. The consequences are severe and more often than not, only those of us at the intersections of these margins know what's coming and how to prevent it. This is the time to center Trans Muslim Palestinian leadership. The time to center Muslim Trans Black and Indigenous leadership. The time to center Trans Palestinian and Trans Black leadership.

The rise of fascism can end with us.

References:
[1] https://navigatingdifferences.com/clarifying-sexual-and-gender-ethics-in-islam/
[2] https://afsc.org/gaza-genocide-companies
[3] https://www.ic3.gov/Media/Y2024/PSA240510

I claim power
in skills
lineages,
emotional intelligence
in moving beyond
fear

there is power in knowing
you have nothing to lose

what will they do to me?
kill me?
please, I'm a death doula
death is the final beginning

why is it
that today
of all days
under an eclipse
shirtless in the
sun, do I feel
at home?

is it astrological?
or is it that today
after nearly 2
years is the most
any strangers have
ever talked to me?

can home ever
be a place we
are not wanted?
if so, are trans
folks ever
home?

the moon drifts
like it did 6 months
ago

barely moving
we are barely
moving

yet the sun &
moon intersect
partially

others walk
around, a loss without
glasses

I wonder if
they feel what I
feel

the rage simmering

yet partially quieting
down

the hunger for
war slowly
releasing

on the way
here, I prayed for
fire

now, underneath
the sun kissing my
skin
I pray for
cleansing from
everything

we are the
world we
deserve

the moon eats
a chunk from
the sun, it
already feels
chillier

I wonder if
they feel it
in tents and
encampments
without food
just the sounds
around them in
Oakland,
Sudan,
Gaza

if they
    -   children & adults
in the
Congo feel the
sacred rocks
cool

I feel my soul
relaxing, tempered

after 6 months
1 year
6 years
76 years
500 years
after, after
always after

I wonder if
they feel it
or if maybe
they don't
feel anything
at all

is pressing the
button, that'll
kill another family
harder? or is it
just as easy
as the family
minutes ago?

may we be
better when the
sun shines its
light on us
once more

perhaps this world is
just a world like any
other

perhaps life is
just to be lived
death is just to
be embraced

my community care
is rageful
anger at systems
that are built to
fail **us**, succeed **them**
benefiting colonizers
and billionaires, one and
the same

I build funds
peer support programs
resource after resource
my rage building
every day

I do not build
for a world that
is generous

I build in a

ravenous society
that extracts
everything from us
our resources, our
labor, our souls

I build to claim
them.

the sun & moon
are both valid
even when we can't
see them

may we all
find solace
in knowing that
we are miniscule
in comparison to
suns & moons
that block us
from themselves
that grant us
grace & unwavering
support, even when
blocked

may we recognize
we are descendants
of stars, although
miniscule in size
colossal in being

our magic
wells of love and

compassion, world
builders and world
destroyers alike
we choose utopia
we claim worlds
we claim our souls

the new moon
ushers in Eid
always

many will say
they must see
the crescent to
verify

tell me why
that when Allah
sends a whole
ass eclipse
to usher in the
new month
they still say we
have not seen
the moon and
will celebrate a
day late

perhaps this is
the perfect metaphor

we witness genocide
after genocide
yet some still ask
if capitalism, white supremacy
settler colonialism
Is bad

asking if there's
a way to save
"israel", "US"
"canada"
as if we have
not always
known

they depart leaving
the eclipse only
three quarters of
the way through
how the privileged
abandon us when
they are tired and
bored

the tiniest of
slivers make the
sun look deformed
she's beautiful and
perfect in her
imperfection

I wonder if the
sun looks at
the mirror of
itself in the
moon and wonders
if she should be
different

my body aches
an atom bomb's
worth of bombs
cascading against
my skin
I do not have
enough bones to
carry every name

there are names
of trans-Palestinians
that will die with me
never able to present
them to the world
never acknowledged
as trans before, during, or after
never again

in some cultures
eclipses are the moon
and sun
lovers
uniting

what unity is needed
to free the world?
to free Falasteen?

may we unite life's
lovers, in moments
stopping the world
eclipsing the past
towards the future

it ends as
i write this
a final dimple
on her right cheek
then it's over

i wonder how many
noticed, how many
pretended it was
all in our heads
looking aside from
social media, the
news, eyes of anti-zionist
family & friends

how many ignored
Hinds dimples and
Zhra's lashes
busy with work
and whatnot

how many will
claim they saw
it anyways?

some will claim
they never knew

Baba's love for
the ocean,
lives in my veins
no matter how
much i begged it
to leave me in
peace.

waves crash,
reminding me of
home, where bombs
generously drop,
gifting everyone
inequitably.

I wonder if
your blood will
ever meet mine
in between oceans
and seas.

I wonder a lot
of things.
will I ever cross
this ocean to your
sea? will I feel
closer to Baba
if I follow his
strokes? Will
I stop hearing
the bombs if
there's no one
left?

may everyone
lost at sea find
home

may this
eclipse be a
foreshadowing of
the end of empire
on turtle island

The Narcissist

our pain is
fetishized
even by the
most pro-palestine
non-palestinians

we are caricatures
breakable stick figures
snapped this way
and that by
supporters and those
who want us entirely
erased, pain & all

fetishization is a tool
of genocide, erasure of
the whole, weaponizing
what remains
our being, our joy
our liberation does
not sell, only our
pain, from the eyes
of our oppressors

they claim our liberation
is held by the masses
when the masses
have never been
right to claim any
of us at all

to say we need
everyone is to
claim that we
are not enough

we will claim
our liberation
regardless

a free Falasteen
is guaranteed

settler colonialism
capitalism
all of empire will
fall

there will be no
israel

canada
australia
united states

you claim to be
more than you can ever
be.

Yet, I am called the narcissist.

Rage

there is something
clawing at the
sides of my mind
a rage I used
to fear

the dark phoenix
destruction that I
find most global
majority trans folks
carry, a terror
of the shadow
parts of us.

aries beckons in
its new moon
demanding an end
to a world that
was always meant
to end.

i'm transported to
being 7, envisioning
creating a robot

suit, over a decade
before seeing iron
man, as large as
godzilla, I would
free Falasteen.

at ten, praying
daily to be the
Mahdi, the one
who will free
us all.

at 17, the
spirit of death
as every friend
was killed and
died. No one
safe, from me.

early 20's, afraid
of any anger,
any raised voices
"terrorist" echoing
all around me
Boston Marathon Bombings
tech school that

feeds arms dealers
why cis straight folks
who only know fear
of me

late 20's
claiming rage as
a tool to build
endless nonprofits
mutual aid funds
dozens of books
rage worn out in
hundreds of planes.

I am meant to
die at 32

at 31 I claim
rage
I want fires
like those that
lit up June 2020
I want screams
that haunt their
nightmares
words that make

them irrelevant

I want justice
this aries moon

then, I want to
replace it all,
build before, during, after

people ask me
about
rest as resistance
joy as resistance

i ask
back
what's rest?
who's joy?

i ask
again
which resistance?
to what?

my
rest
is
resistance
because it has
never been

permitted

my
joy
is
resistance
because it
has been criminalized

my resistance
is to claim
a world where
that is no longer
the case

where my people
any people
can rest without
genocide at our
doorsteps
where my people
can be joyful without
being kidnapped, trafficked,
killed

our joy, our rest

is not the same
when your joy and rest
have always been accessible

just because
you don't know
how to feel joy and how to
rest doesn't change
that

it is not the
world that
creates literature
it is literature
that builds the
world

what worlds are
you building?

part 1
expansion

part 2
fill in the expansion
with community & beauty

Part 3
ascend beyond
the expansion

the expansion is
not a bubble
it is a part of
who we are

we are the
expansion
we transcend
the physical &

metaphysical

somehow i am still
moving towards who
I have always
needed to be.

I have fallen
in love more
times in the
last 6 months
than the last
31 years combined

they will come
for us
in policy
in removing our
existence from books
and curricula

they will try
to erase us

Palestine is a
queer & trans
issue

the genocide of
trans people in
the global north
has been in the
works for years
as the genocides of
indigenous folks

continues
in Falasteen, Sudan,
the Congo,
here, there
everywhere in
between
settler colonialism
anywhere is genocide
everywhere

queerness is inherently
about marginalization
there is no queer
liberation without
the liberation of everyone
marginalized

the right wing
white Christian nationalists
spend billions
building an army
from global south
soldiers
always white generals

when fascism

claims the north
the liberals will claim
it was those who
refused to believe
genocide is the lesser
of two evils

how easy it is to
live in a liberated world...

how easy it is for
folks to pretend otherwise...

To be queer, part 1

is to be
displaced
wandering between
constellations of
pain and fabulousness
majesty and abandonment

to be queer
is to be
utopian
believing in a
world most find
off putting
impossible they say

to be queer
is to be incomplete
searching for the
missing pieces
found only in
heaven

to be queer
is to be unsafe

always - everywhere
except in space
where queerness
is all there is

to be queer
is to yearn for
an end
to queerness
a world
without marginalization

to be queer
is to be different
ostracized and
oppressed are
the best case
scenarios

to be queer
is not a flavor
or hair dye
it is death
the waiting for
murder

to be queer
is to rise above
leaving behind
loved ones
family, friends
even ourselves

to be queer
is to be

they claim
our bodies
harvesting organs,
bone marrow

even dead they envy
us, peeling back
our skin,
searching

never knowing
desecrated
poppies
will never
guide them
home

as we enter
the age of
fascism
may we still
remember we are
worthy & will
find liberation
always

I am a culture worker

I pride myself in being kind, not nice. I will not waste time with nonsense. I will not speak to you directly if you can not recognize how our survival is connected. I will tell you your question is basic and I will offer a worthy question that moves past the basics. I will create community care pathways. I will mention, educate, train, and support everywhere I can. You will not waste my time though, for the energy it takes me to try to convince a single zionist that they are absolute trash I will have finished writing this book and it will already be in stores. You are not my priority. I will tell you that I am here to make you irrelevant, remove any harm you may cause and then and only then may we engage in a conversation. You are not my priority.

I create for me, first and foremost, and when I say I create for me I am saying I create for folks who look and feel like I do, who are global majority, queer, trans, neurodiverse, disabled, global south citizens, those who know poverty, houselessness, and food insecurity intimately. I speak to the mad, those like me and others who expand what is real everyday.

I am a culture worker. At 12 painting, sketching, weaving novels, always recognizing that art is culture and culture is transformative. Although I grew up separate from a larger Palestinian community, I have always known that my people are world builders, poetry a pillar of worldbuilding that transcends the worst atrocities of settler colonialism.

At 13 I understood that art is to be celebrated, but only within the confines of a time and place where it is robbed of its transformative and world-building capacity. If I had gone to art school – I am grateful I did not – I believe I would have taken on more of the destructive methodology of technical perfection instead of the methodology that art is always perfect and the imperfections determine whether or not art is worldbuilding.

A culture worker is not an artist. A culture worker practices art, but they are a weaver of culture, an agent of transformation, an architect of the future. If art is worldbuilding, then culture workers are those of us who expand that reality beyond possibility. Anyone can write, draw, play instruments; these are technical skill sets. Even when it comes to raw talent, an individual may be technically the greatest artist there is, but if the art does not move us beyond, then it is only art, not a culturally transformative form of existence. It is not culture work.

The description above makes it seem like culture workers are always moving us towards liberation, but like most roles in existence, we can move towards liberation or we can move towards fascism (if we were to simplify into a binary). Fascist culture workers exist all around us, doing the fascist state's work, either paid or unpaid. We have always witnessed art that harms communities instead of elevating them. Hollywood is a perfect example of fascist culture work. Hollywood is a tool to strengthen and maintain systems of oppression and the status quo.

"This sentence about hollywood is challenging my long-held perspective that more diverse voices need to be working in that town, and puts my frustrations with how slowly that's been moving into new perspective: of course it's moving slowly, the overall culture of hollywood would prefer not to be challenged by more diverse voices and will resist that as long as possible! Now I'm thinking about the barbie movie with this lens, in combination with something from the other essay in this book: how the elite, the establishment will elevate some for the illusion of progress and to distract from the effects of their divide and conquer strategy." - Mays Salamah, line editor of essays, *Desecrated Poppies*.

Over the last several years I have been reflecting on publishing and worldbuilding. Everything in our day to day realities has already been captured in literature. I wondered, who owns our stories? When nearly every decision maker in publishing is not us.

If I went to a large publisher telling them I would like to write a memoir about how transphobic Muslim Palestinians are, I would receive a six-figure book deal immediately. If I tell them that my dad prays in the mosque five times a day and my mom wears a hijab and knows the quran and I myself pray five times a day and we're cute - our relationship stronger because I am all I am and my parents wholeheartedly accept, not understanding why it's a big deal that we're in a fabulous relationship - I would not be given anything. In fact, I would most likely be censored.

We often frame this in terms of money: it wouldn't sell, many would say, but we know that is a lie. There is a hunger for stories of love and acceptance, a hunger for joy, a hunger for wellness. Arguably, the latter book would sell better. It will not be sold because it is worldbuilding and that is a vision of the world that is counter to the fascist culture work the world's elites are investing in. I write this recognizing the immense privilege I have; not everyone has the option to assimilate into fascism, even if only temporarily, for survival or to achieve a goal.

I have always been doing community work.

Belonging has been my love language since my first traumatic memory at 22 months old and I decided to belong by dissociating.

My autism has gifted me with an awareness of systems of oppression from some of my very first memories. I knew islamophobia, anti-Palestinian hatred, ableism, and anti-poverty from about three years old. These systems were easy to understand in my birth country, Jordan.

Then, moving to what's known as Arizona I quickly learned macro-violence due to systems of oppression. I learned white supremacy at six when every white person I came in contact with either released dogs at me and my family in parks, followed us around in stores, or called the cops on us for existing.

Oppression moved from a feeling in Jordan to a direct survival threat in what's known as the United States. This is a difference that many in the Global North can not comprehend, especially in settler colonial states. Within settler colonial states – such as what's known as the united states and canada or the Zionist State (all places I hope no longer exist by the time you read this) – it is as if you are in a meat grinder. You do not know when the grinding occurs, but you are there.

In many ways, oppression in the Global South is about witnessing and feeling, engaging with systems of oppression, but in many ways the blade is not on your throat the entire time like it is in these settler colonial states. This assessment is obviously limited, for the Global South is large, but it is from visiting over 40 global south countries and nearly 30 global north, and this has been my experience. At the very least, when the global south kills you as a direct form of oppression you are free to die. If I am killed in Jordan by the state – a state that operates as a neo-colony for the British, Canadians, and Americans, my family will be able to bury me with ease. They will not get into debt to return me to the soil I came from. When I am killed in what's known as the United States I am only buried after endless paperwork, tens of thousands in burial fees, medical bills, and taxes that I do not have. They oppress us in life and then, when the meat is ground they repackage us and sell us to capitalism, one final time (if we're lucky).

The weight of oppression is not something you can hide from or avoid in settler colonial states, it is always permeating. From living in 9 countries, across various forms of oppressive systems, it is in settler colonial states that I feel this most, as soon as I land and as soon as I depart. Like the white violence of my childhood, there is no protection. Again, I also honor my privilege, for if I was a black child with the same experiences, I would most definitely have been killed.

But I am not black, so despite having guns pointed at me by cops that I have always known are not there for non-cis straight rich white folks, my body has not been pierced by a hundred bullets because whiteness demands the assassination of black bodies to maintain capitalism.

Instead, I was born a Trans Palestinian, born into displacement, three generations' worth at the time. Growing up in Arizona you may have seen elements of my Sudanese ancestry, but after over a decade between New England, Switzerland, Ireland, and the two years of Canada in my adolescence, you are more likely to connect me with my Palestinian olive skin.

Born into displacement, months after my parents were displaced again, this time from Kuwait after the gulf war, meant that I was also born into community care. Our community care was not a cute thing to have, it was not something we had to have a conversation about and set a constitution of values to work together. True community care for us is simple: if we do not automatically show up for one another we all die.

Moving to Arizona, this care became more visible, a community of displaced immigrants and Black American Muslims still living in the oppression of displacement from 400 years earlier. Our community knew how to take care of one another, and for that I'm grateful. My community showed up for one another, and nearly every weekend we were on the streets of Phoenix in protest against various injustices around the world.

Then 9/11 happened. Our mosque was vandalized prior to 9/11 and immediately after. In fact, most of my personal negative experiences with white non-Muslims in Arizona happened prior to 9/11.

Community members disappeared, not a single family untapped by the FBI. I spoke to the FBI for the first time when I was 10. Although ordinarily quiet, at 10 I knew how to act around the two white officers who came into our house on Hardy St. I remember Mama's eyes wondering, fearful of what I'd say – fearful of words they would twist before pulling the knife, but I understood, I have always understood.

Organizing died, the lighter skinned folks moved towards capitalism and whiteness, leaving my family and our black community behind.

We left, the bridge between us gone, replaced by another settler colonial state – Canada.

Canada's evil makes it unremarkable and not worthy to mention beyond this. I moved towards art in Canada. Like everything else in my life, it starts and ends with survival.

I wanted to run away, is the truth. J.K. Rowling had made a billion dollars by then. Writing novels was my escape. One of my favorite things in life is seeing the white mediocrity of J.K. Rowling and having the confidence as a 13-year-old trans fabulous person to do better. May every trans child have the confidence that survival forced into my being.

Beyond that, my art has always been about cultural transformation, from the speech I gave about bombs dropping and displacement at 13, to art in my 8th grade yearbook, to putting my baby sister's photo as my own baby photo as a statement that some of us do not have the privilege of baby photos, to the baggy clothes I hated in high school but wore anyway to overturn the school uniform within days, to working with Global Majority Queer and Trans artists to start conversations and belong, to creating art space, to filling gaps within artist offerings, to storytelling starting at 19, to pushing even after the death threats started, to building transformative justice pathways when the TERFS tried to cancel me, to building non-profits, to starting peer support programs in manufacturing facilities, to bringing engineering to mental health and social sciences, to every released article and book, to every hour training, to every speaking engagement, to...

Mama says I have always lived my life for everyone else. I am a culture worker. I matter. I matter as an extension of transformation and a vision of society that moves us to liberation, always.

Culture work is about strategy, a deep and profound understanding, and in my opinion a fight for survival. In a world where moving towards thriving is the goal, culture work asks us to claim a foundation built on survival that I wish to center. It is our connection with our survival that allows us to thrive and be liberatory culture workers. I am effective at what I do because I have lived through it. I know we do not have time, I know how the tides shift, how public opinion and those in power lose interest, I know the need to act immediately and build infrastructure at the same time. I have timelines down to a science, when interest is lost, when conflict starts, when conflict is unaddressed and tears things apart, I know how to support the culture workers on the frontlines, I know how to move resources, I know how to pivot and shift and predict. I know how to survive because I have had to survive these systems for generations. Survival is built into my DNA.

Culture work did not begin with us; for many of us it transcends time and space. My paternal grandfather told stories through the calluses on his farming hands. My maternal grandfather wove stories of salons and gatherings. My paternal grandmother weaves stories through her early stage dementia, capturing memories previously lost to time. My maternal grandmother weaves me bedtime stories as we near her 30th death anniversary. I am a story that is descended from storytellers.

My organizing, my engineering, my visual art, my writing are all part of my culture work. Those of us in this work know that our work is effective not because we know how to work, rather it is because we are culture.

I am a transformative being regardless of any other circumstances (yes, I am a leo(x4)). It is not my words, my makeup, or fabulous outfits that make people stop. I can look like the most basic cis person and I will be noticed.

We are all transformative beings, some of us are aware of this, and know that for our communities' survival we must use that power as culture workers. We always have the choice to walk away, to move towards assimilation (as false as it is). The calls of liberation are louder, we are louder.

These days, I am a culture worker. I supervise a team of eleven at MASGD, I have launched a queer and trans muslim peer line, I mentor countless other culture workers, I have had over 50 speaking events in seven and a half months of the zionist genocide in Gaza, I have published a poetry book and the works of 17 others, I have redistributed over $200,000, I have connected others with funding and resources up to half a million dollars. All incredible things. AND the largest chunk of work is what lies beneath them all.

My community care is not policed, I will not ask questions, I will find money, and when I find it, it is redistributed. No questions, no proof beyond. Especially with organizers, I work to shift culture away from scarcity, sending money for DJ sets, massages, and breathing room within capitalism. One of my greatest joys is seeing this culture shift in action. An organizer who I have supported with this culture shift told me that they are redistributing money for rent and bought a guitar for someone who is also receiving rent support. Culture shifts in knowing that conflict does not have to destroy us, that nothing is wasted, that we build with others who can acknowledge that our survival is connected, that we are worthy of someone flying across the planet for us, that we can and should be seen. That we are valid. That we are transformation.

And it is our culture, we as culture, that disrupts fascism. The iconic Yalini Dream shares that culture workers are the anti-fascist path forward. We are the path forward. Fascism will come, if not here somewhere else. We are the antidote everywhere.

We will be punished and we will be assassinated when they want to hijack our being. Nothing is wasted. Our punishment and murder serving to build a world free of fascism.

I look forward to being wrong someday, it's not my fault it rarely happens. So prove me wrong, build me a world free of fascism, where fascism never rises, where my people (all people) live in liberation.

May I be proven wrong soon.

I would

hi,
I say and you stare out
lifeless eyes filled with
an intensity I rarely
noticed when I was you
excited, devoted, inspired
you are motivation
how my heart aches
for you

I'd go
to the hospital with you
hug you on the way
tell you I love you
that I'll be the first
you see when you
walk out

I'd take you
to a retreat where
they can't find you

I'd try
to stop the harm

before it happened
stop them
protect you
if I can't I will
be there to hold you

I'd listen
to every word
said and unsaid
scream with you
shatter things that need
to be

I'd cry
with you
wiping your tears
as I hold on to every
part of you
every part I love

***

why didn't
anyone really help?

why was
I disposable?

why did
I trust them?

why did
I think I could have a family?

why?
why me?

I gave them
so much of me

why was
I not enough?

I feel so tired
sleepy

I want it
to end

will you
help me?

***

I would
hold you endlessly

I would
caress your cheek

I would
hum a lullaby for sleep

I would
cook and clean

I would
get you housing

I would
sleep with you in the car

I would
read to you

I would
make you tea

I would
help you move

I would
love you, still and forever

I would
help you get a new job

I would
get you a break

I would
tell you it's not your fault

I would
tell you you're valid, worthy of everything

I would
love and hold you
protect you and help you pick up the
pieces

I claim all
of me
because no
one ever has

no one
said I am
everything
because I
am

I celebrate all
of me
because no one
has celebrated
me

I was a quiet
child
selective mutism
built from
trauma and autism
and my silence
was celebrated

I was a good

student
math and science
my forte
I was honored
for good grades
that tore the
seams of my
mind

I was an
artist
sketching in
math and writing
novels in
english
they tried to catch
me off guard
I won awards
anyways

I was a motivated
organizer
they preyed off
eighty hour
work weeks
tossed aside

when I began
claiming
me

I was
alone
when the pills
and hospitals
came
when they asked
where I was going
and I said my
car is the only
safety I
have ever known
in Walmart
parking lots
cops creeping
from every direction

I was a caring
sibling
when I flew oceans
to sit by hospital
beds
paying tuition

and walking home
frostbite eating
my toes
told to censor
everything I am
because children
will ask
questions

I was a
lover
when I put my needs
aside for theirs
one-sided compromises
a predator when I
said no
to marriage
to sex
to relationships

I claim everything
because only I
claim without
demanding a return
on investment

so I stand
on stages
in front of thousands
and shine my own
light

you will all
fade with time
I will grow old
in time
I will love
every ache
every wrinkle

demanding nothing
but being

I am whole
that is
all

there's a world
beyond the fascism
where justice is
called, ushering
an age of liberation
may we be of
the shuhadah
who inspire
justice
not one of the
dead who stood
by as the fires
ravaged the world

Saturn enters aries
soon
fires will rage
the world remade

she said
it is not about
who wins an election
or who you vote for
it is about building
infrastructure to
respond to whatever
comes

I say
make them irrelevant
their power meaningless
harmless
then we talk

how can we build
together when you have
power over me?
power you don't
acknowledge?

they think
their money &
privilege will save
them from the
fascism they
nurtured

the lesser of evils
is the breeding ground
for the greatest
evil

do you benefit
from fascism?

the handmaid's tale
tells yt women they
are the ultimate
victims of fascism
as Black, Indigenous,
disabled, and trans
people are genocided

the yt gays of
castro claim
unhappy marriages
saved them
as trans children
disappear from the
world
as black trans women
can not afford their
burial ground.

the light skinned
in tech will think
their lives are on
the line, as they
build infrastructure
to wipe us all out
wondering if a pay
cut is worth it,
never quite saying
that the rest of us
are not

the non-trans queers
will claim they
will lose their
base if they center
us, that they are
queer, can not possibly be queerphobic
as they sustain the breeding
ground for our end

you can not be
pro-palestine and
anti-black
anti-indigenous
anti-poor
anti-disabled
anti-trans
at the same time

you can pretend
but you can not
claim liberation
while feeding
fascism

it is only
a matter of time
when the beast
you fed grows and
hunts you down
be very afraid

Palestine & transness
have many things
in common
not least of which
is that both are
weaponized to create
fascist policy
when we fall fascism begins

soon, they'll forget
the faces in the rubble
that could not have been
more than a few years old
lost in the brown sea
of our lives

brown seas are 'dirty'
they say and we wonder
if maybe they're right
those who define color
who pollute and weave new
paths away from old

I wonder how I believed
them. was it the fourth grade
teacher? who taught me Palestinians
are only white and I am not? was it
umm H? who never said so but
believed money could save
us. was it British flight attendants?

who did not know how to care
for a six year old.
was it me? them?

in a life of war and displacement
the thing I am ashamed of
most is wanting to be
a Derik

we talk about a queer Muslim trip
to Palestine, about a farm we own
a small Palestine anywhere
I wonder who will be willing
to go to rebuild when it's free
or if people will make the same excuses

my last new beginning will be home

there is no
metaphor for you - you
are lowest of creation

my ancestors stare
sternly above me
martyrs, witnessing
me, my queerness and
my transness

I hear whispers
others saying they
would be ashamed
they say nothing
in response

I wait
they stare
I yearn for
the queer and trans
ancestors
who would tell
the voices
they have no home
here

I forget
what it was like
driving for
eighteen months
freezing in my
car, cops harassing
me, terrified of the
day
and night

I forget
what it was like
to sleep on park
benches
men creeping and
asking if I wanted
a place to rest

I forget
what it was like
to watch war after war

new war
cycles witnessed
again and again

I forget
what it was like
to taste air
as if it were
filled with
nutrients

I forget
what it was like
to sneak into houses
for a packet of magi and
stale crackers no one
will miss

I forget
what it was like
in line for SNAP
the smell of shame
lingers

I forget
what it was like

when the Canadian immigration officer
came into the
waiting room
screaming at my
mom
I forget
what it is like
to witness another
genocide, knowing
we do not matter
to most

I forget
most things
it's a miracle
I remember
at all

I've had to
justify my transness
everyday of
every life

within the broader
LGBTQ+ community
within the Muslim
the Palestinian
the disabled
the everything
all communities asking
more than they are
entitled to

my identities are seen
to be at odds with each other
by people who are so limited
in their capacity to hold

I am asked to not
"be political"
when my existence
is political

I am expected
to bridge the divide
of where we need to be
and where we are
fought by everyone
in the process
deemed ungrateful
always

I am of Sudanese
descent from my dad's side
Armenian from my mom's
entirely Palestinian
racism denying one, two,
or three and that's before
the autistic transness
is introduced

I link the two
because according
to society my transness

is of repression, assault, trauma
or something else
that explains away and makes
me make sense

but I don't make sense
there is no amount
of trying that will make
sense of identities
that claim one another
cannibalizing
in spite of the constant
demand to make them
make sense

my people are being
brutally killed
legacy of genocide
four generations old
my black family members
my trans family members
my Armenian family members
my autistic family members
all gone in an instant
within media blackouts
names only found

in lists denied by
leaders of the "free world"
only "free" because we "die"
as if we were not killed
here, there, everywhere
in between
I have lost more
family and friends
in six weeks
than I can name

I have been robbed of more
trans lives
than I have in my
life today

make that
make sense

still everyday
I get messages
from LGBTQ+ people
telling me my people
are the ones who would
murder me

I would give anything
to be murdered at home
instead of slowly killed
by whiteness that has claimed
your marginalization
still, you try
to make me
make sense

someday
you will have
capacity for everything
you can be
then, and only then
I will
make sense

my kuffiyeh sits
upon my head
a crown
gleaming in
white and black
black and blue
green and brown
endless colors
for we are
the original
rainbow
there is no pride
without us
bleeding in the sun
on every screen
to create it

they say
queerness is the
source of pride
but sex has never

actually been the
issue
it has
always been the
lack of white and wealth
Christianity ruling above
the stolen god didn't
look like us

they thought
the land was starved
of blood and knew theirs
wasn't worthy

I used to say
my family is
displaced from
two wars
not realizing
war is not three
generations long
how many wars
must one survive
before they all
become the same
one?

it's not
fair
they say
as if fair
hadn't always
meant white
maybe if we
bleached our eyes
we'd look like
their god
even then
we'd be sacrificed like
he was

Right now

to be Palestinian
is to be on the verge
of crying
all the time

to be Palestinian
is to be trying to
figure out a way
to die with your
people

to be Palestinian
is to withdraw
from people and places
that can't grasp
your existence

to be Palestinian
is to wonder if
you'll ever go
home

to be Palestinian
is to be asked

to celebrate your
oppressors

to be Palestinian
is to be told
you're demanding
too much too fast
"wait" they say

to be Palestinian
is to write poetry
on every road
to avoid yelling at
everyone

to be Palestinian
is to worry you might
be deported
unsure to where

to be Palestinian
is to have everyone
think you're
breaking
when you've never
been whole

to be Palestinian
is to believe in
a free Palestine
even when they
tell us it's
impossible

to be Palestinian
is to resist
until the world
is ready to hold
us

to be a trans Palestinian
is to be everything
everything

they say,
God said
we are the worst
in creation.

have they not witnessed genocide?
have they not glimpsed whiteness?
have they not met capitalism?
have they not seen themselves?

can I get
a life back
for every follower?

I flirt with him
he flirts back
he's from Yaffa, he says
part of the ones who went
southwest instead of
southeast

we're not much different
similar age
despite the bombs on
his end, his smile
shines brighter than
mine

I do what I
can, I say
knowing he's the last
one I know alive

when I die
Mama will wail
he'll scream
throw himself on
my grave
buried between Muslims
if they'll let me

Mama will cry
they'll say she
was never the same

Baba will hide
in his room
a sister will sneak
in witnessing
what broke when his
own dad died

sisters will cry
in their own ways

some radicalized
some numb
maybe it'll bring them
closer, maybe not

friends will wonder why
asking if there were signs
ignoring dozens of videos
mapping death threats
assassinated by the govt
in the end
similarly, some radicalized
some numb
the ones who weren't
worthy will name
children after me
raising them into
whiteness and capitalism

it'll be worse
for you
wondering what I
was actually like
a myth, an icon
tears for someone
you may have met once

from the Internet you'd known

then, everything
moves, shifts
flattens and launches
into space
the world forgets
replacing me with
who they want

food for whiteness
fuel for capitalism
forgotten when
revolution arrives

at peace
at home
always

you elevate
me
thoughts materializing
profound quotes
you repeat back
on stages
where we can laugh
as I claim their
profoundness

community elevates
we are more
together
the opposite
can never be true

you live in
theoretical
terror

we live without
blood and bones
crushed under your
bulldozers and tanks

6 months
beckoned by an
eclipse

as the world
bathes in darkness
we watch stars
colliding with
friends' homes
family, no longer
recognizable

it started with
a ring of fire
it ends in
totality

and the world
goes on
from a no longer
visible Sudan

from a genocide
that birthed another
this phone I write
on haunted by the
child whose life
gave it birth
unnecessarily

has it ever been
necessary?
how envious you
must be of those
of us who know
it has never been

you feed
when there has always
been enough

how envious you
must be to know
that you take from us
yet are the only ones
whole

Birthing

6 months
of denial and erasure
gaslighting and nightmares
that won't sleep
are they still
sleeping when we
can't piece together
body parts?

6 months
told I'll be thrown
off buildings
that no longer
exist

6 months
$150,000 raised
distributed
knowing money won't
fix this

6 months
writing poetry
on a phone that

Congolese people are
genocided for

6 months
invisible, alone
waiting for
the end

6 months
and a day
our Sumoud is
everlasting by
definition

do i give
others what they
want because
I believe I can't get
what I want?

if I allowed myself
I'd admit to wanting a
home
a couple of bedrooms
a kitchen we can dance
in, the smell of freshly baked
chocolate chip cookies
baked into the walls
Nina Simone in
the background

I'd admit to wanting a
partner
whose hands fit mine
warm cuddles even when
it's too hot out
your sweat and mine

I'd admit to wanting a
garden
one of every tree

like Seedos where
ancestors come and visit me
and mine

I'd admit to wanting a
dog
a sheep, even a goat
some cats
life surrounding us
always

I'd admit to wanting a
child
or children that are ours
adopted through
time

I'd admit to wanting a
life
friends, time to just be
not only time to
react

instead, I'm on a plane
two this morning
another later

thousands of miles
stretching in every
direction
hoping that when I
land Falasteen
is free
hoping when I
land someone else
is doing community
care
hoping when I
land trans people
won't be murdered
anymore
hoping when I
land the parts of
me yearning and willing
to admit are still
here

that I'm still
here

they hate us
because we remind
them of the divine and
they realize they're nothing
like Them

they envy us
because we're the
essence of the divine and
they Feel helpless in their
void

they kill us
because it's the
closest to the divine
they could ever
get

they hate us
they envy us
they kill us

the result is
the same

we are hated
we are envied
we are murdered

we are divine

I do not
feel sorry
for myself
yearnings and dreams
that can not be
today
I mourn a world
we deserved
not a single life
that could have been
in this world
I regret nothing
I resent nothing

I would rather always
show up
building the world
we deserve than
standing by as oppression
rises into fascism

?

how?
do?
you?
share?
an?
image?
of?
children?
about?
to?
die?
deleting?
it?
realizing?
they?
were?
the?
wrong?
children?

how awful it must be to be you

Field

there's a field
of wheatgrass and love
where the parts of all I am
converge in constellations
of home
it is a physical place I have
visited in time
peed my pants from sheer joy
developed over time and lost
taken to the afterlife
when Seedo died
now it lives in my mind

countless moons hover above
a fig tree holds the universe
underneath a lantern filled with
the cosmos with a smokeless
flame burning from the purest
olive oil not of this world
here I am everything
all the possibilities that ever
were and will be
here lies Utopia beneath and through
above and beyond

there is no me
there is only oneness
this is home

they say nice tan
I don't know how to explain
that my melanin was a gift
returned from the sun
no tan lines underneath
the fabulous garments
I wear

how do I explain that
as soon as the sun hits my
skin my ancestors remember me
embracing all I am

I remember in grade school
we'd compete to figure out
who was the whitest
of course it was always the
kids with a white parent

no one told us
it's okay to be brown

and black in Islamic school
the Levantian teachers pitting
us against one another
denying our identities if we
weren't light enough
the half white Palestinian
was the only permitted Palestinian
to the Palestinian teachers
I was too dark to be
Palestinian
so I stopped being anything
just a dark brown genderless
child
invisible and disposable
except in the ways I made
for myself
then, robbed of my melanin
I became too light to be
of color and too dark to be
anywhere near white
my skin forgotten
my ancestry lost
until I claimed it
without validation

I am queer

not only due to gender
and orientation
I am queer
invisible between
shades of brown
too dark too light
the sun and the moon
in endless cycles
fuck your validation
I want to say
I never desired it but
that's not true
I wonder what a childhood
where I am held
would have been like
or a world where I am held
even as an adult

To be queer, part 2

to be queer
is to glimmer
in starhood
lighting every crevice
in a society that knows
our power
aiming to dim what is
undimmable

to be queer
is to fly
feet never leaving
or touching the ground
embracing gravity
like an extension
of grace and warmth
caressed and held

to be queer
is to be visible
in realms beyond
what society pretends
to know
deeming us invisible and hypervisible

to be queer
is to be joy
in bodies and societies
unequipped to carry
transcendental enjoyment
conceived from stardust

to be queer
is to be the envy of stars
and celestial bodies
who recognize
angels bowing to the
endlessness
within us

within me
within you

textiles can't capture
the fabrics that yearn to
drape this body
languages don't begin
to comprehend my voice

recognition of stardust
is a simplification that can't
begin to capture what stars are
what I am

if you believe
that the soul of the divine
flows through humanity
how can you hate us?
how can you hate yourself?
how can you hate me?

I am divine
I am stardust
I.AM.PHOENIX
Xxx

I would
field
rage
right now
to be queer,
to be queer
birthing
the narcissist

I float
on a call
with other QTM
we go from immense pain
unabashed grief
to laughing over
white nonsense
the two intersect
relief of validation
keeping us afloat
at rest
in community

death threats bleed
into one another
starting with Palestine
ending with transness
a pendulum that doesn't
know how to stop
what is an acceptable number
of death threats a day?

I haven't written
a poem in days
it feels...
I feel....
vacant
like someone Marie
Kondo'd my insides
but instead left
nothing at all

the NYC subway
sways, as if lost
swimming in a sea
lost to global warming

it's Nakba Day
as if the Nakba
was one day
one day, not
thirty years
as if colonizers

did not switch
places, again, and again
Falasteen erased
again and again

to imagine a day
when 700,000 leave
their homes is to imagine
a day when there was
no more Gaza
as if seven months of
genocide never existed

the Nakba is
30 years of genocide
calculated, structured
British inspired
Zionist enacted
American supported

are multiple genocides
that never end
considered just
one?

they stare at me

in my kuffiyeh
guarding my crown
my Palestinian shirt
shining
purple and white makeup
they stare and I know
their grandparents stared
as mine were
displaced on this
Nakba Day

this might be
the last poem
I write on
paper, my veins
bulging, fingers
tightening, even my
thumb is in pain

there might come
a day when I
can no longer move
my fingers or use my
lips to speak

on that day i will
find other ways to
speak, to write,
to move towards
liberation

Acknowledgments

Immense gratitude goes out to the culture workers at the forefront of building a world where fascism is not around the corner. A heartfelt thank you to Yalini Dream, Seema Yasmin, Eman Abdelhadi, Randa Jarrar, Hannah Moushabeck, Sara Ramirez, Indya Moore, Kirill Staklo, Firas Nasr, Hamzeh Daoud, Fayzan Gowani, Marcelle Afram, Maya Ghanem, Safae, Jack, Noon, Gabriel Arkles, Cat Knarr, Xaytoun, Mama Ganuush, Ira X and many others who are paving the way.

Special thanks to Ave Agni for their thoughtful insights and reflections!

A sincere thank you to Michael Colgan for being a visionary Virgo who can see the structure in my work even before I can!

Acknowledgments to the Trans Muslim Liberation Group at MASGD, who came together after this book was written to issue a report about this very topic, making it more accessible.

Gratitude extends to the organizers who have planned dozens of events, allowing me to speak about Palestine and raise funds for queer and trans Palestinians in Gaza.

Thanks to Abilities Dance Boston for bringing my life to life through dance! Appreciation to Ellice, Cassandre, Dara, Claire, Lizbeth, Andrew, and the rest of the dancers and team who bring stories to life with every performance.

A heartfelt thank you to my sisters, Aya, Dana, and Nada, who are always supporting my work. Thank you also to my parents, who may not always understand why the world mistreats anyone.

Special thanks to Andrea Ramos Campos for the continued support and solidarity, helping bring all my work to life.

A big thank you to Mar, Angel, Sam from Bloom Collective, Xtal Azul, and Gaia for supporting me in creating the first trans Palestinian memorial for the trans Palestinians who have been killed in Gaza since October 7th as part of the National Queer Arts festival .

Thank you to Cara and Jessa, who launched and operate the Siren and Deathling Fund that has helped support dozens of queer and trans individuals most impacted by genocide. Additionally, thank you to Zara, Jam, Shiv, Cloud, Allegra, Joy, Bambi and everyone else who has helped with the fabulous book launches and fundraising events to support this work.

Thank you to the organizers that gave their time and energy to our events. This is by no means all of you, but to name a few: Jekksyn, Nour Lofty, Gabriel, Walid, Rachel, Nisha, Aisha, Annie, Yazzie, Shweta, Ananas, Samantha Parks, BA Thomas, Fox Ray, Mayx.

Thank you to the student leaders of the encampments for a free Palestine, particular gratitude to the students at Pomona College, Yale, UMASS, University of New York Albany, University of New York Syracuse, University of California Berkeley.

Thank you to these amazing community spaces for hosting me on my book tours: Lucy Parsons Center, So & So Books, Firestorm books, Tranzmission, Pilsen Community Books, Under the Umbrella

Books, Salon Kawakib, Luya Poetry, Small Format Cafe, Possible Futures, Semilla Cafe, Blue Stockings, Radically Fit, Busboys & Poets, Atamian Hovsepian Curatorial Practice, Medicine for Nightmares, Queer Bedtime Stories, The Majestic Saloon, Nerd Dungeon, Making Worlds Bookstore, Queer Arts Featured, Moments Coop, Cone Shape Top, Eli Tea Bar, Salon Kawakib, Queer Everything Podcast, Abolition Transmission, Queer Arab Podcast, According to Weeze Podcast.

Immense gratitude to everyone conducting work that may never be witnessed but is felt every day!

About the Author

Yaffa (they/she) is an acclaimed disabled, autistic, trans, queer, Muslim, and indigenous Palestinian. Mx. Yaffa is the Executive Director of Muslim Alliance for Sexual and Gender Diversity (MASGD), as well as the founder of several non-profits and community projects.

Yaffa has been actively running mutual aid and community care networks for over 15 years across continents, responding to large-scale disasters such as the Syrian Revolution, COVID-19, and ongoing genocides in Palestine, Sudan, Armenia, and elsewhere. Currently, Yaffa leads three mutual aid efforts: for queer and trans Palestinians in Palestine, for queer and trans people worldwide most impacted by genocide, and for queer and trans people living in the United States most affected by genocide, connecting individuals with over $200,000 in funding for immediate needs.

Mx. Yaffa serves as a death and birthing doula and peer support specialist, working with individuals who lack access to traditional care pathways.

Yaffa is also a visual artist and writer. "Blood Orange," a poetry collection about genocide, displacement, and hope is now available. They are the editor of "Inara" a queer and trans-Palestinian Utopia anthology envisioning a Free Falasteen.

Mx. Yaffa is a storyteller and an equity and transformation consultant, having shared their story with over 175,000 audience members at speaking events globally since 2012.

About Meraj Publishing

Meraj Publishing is a Trans and Queer Muslim publishing house that centers TQM voices from the global majority, with a focus on Palestinian and Black Authors. Recognizing the vast inequities in the publishing industry, we aim to enable TQM individuals from the global majority to fully own our stories. Meraj prioritizes stories that focus on building utopia, hope, love, spirituality, and belonging. Meraj Publishing is entirely run and operated by the TQM global majority.

www.ingramcontent.com/pod-product-compliance
Lightning Source LLC
Chambersburg PA
CBHW071700170426
43195CB00039B/2397